# INTJ: 21 Career Choices for an INTJ

*By Alan Holmes*

# Contents

## INTJ: Introverted, Intuitive, Thinking, Judgment – How This Affects Career Choice

The secretive genius; the brilliant lone wolf. These phrases are often used to describe the INTJ, one of the most rare personality types. We can be simultaneously grateful and regretful that there aren't more of these masterminds in the world. Grateful, because should they turn their extraordinary talents for evil, the rest of us would have some kind of time trying to keep up and neutralize their schemes. Yet we can feel a degree of regret that there aren't more of these personality traits in society, because the marriage of creativity, analysis and organization is one which continuously drives technology forward, especially when they are making it their life's work to create things so that they work better. Think of them as the type who designs the safest air bags on the market or who not only studies black holes but writes articles for popular science magazines, making the topic accessible to non-scientists. INTJs seek not only to understand a subject, but also to master it, and they want to do so on their own terms.

They are driven, yet prefer to work alone; what they do in their careers often benefits many, but their thinking is more facts-based, rather than emotional, and they rank among the top-two personality types with the highest average salary. How can such individuals as these exist? Here is a breakdown of the four personality aspects which makes INTJs who they are.

1

They are:

## Introverted

Whether or not they prefer sciences or the arts, introverts prefer to work alone or in very small groups. In the case of INTJs, this is often because other team members are found wanting in competence, and are viewed as a threat to the overall productivity of the group. INTJs, given a choice, would rather work independently, as they get their "buzz" of energy from time spent alone in their own thoughts, working themselves into a fever pitch of excitement or enthusiasm as their revelations pan out. They are also serious thinkers, preferring to tackle problems from an intellectual perspective, rather than a hands-on approach. Perhaps they could work in a busy and densely populated office, but only if they have space removed from most of the hustle and bustle, and they aren't subject to frequent interruptions.

## Intuitive

Their intuitive trait is what drives them to want to understand and demystify complex and often abstract problems or theories. INTJs don't take a job in engineering because they think math and physics classes are the best way to coast through college and will lead to easy money; they genuinely love the puzzle, and that is all their intuitive aspect talking. It also informs their willingness to try new approaches. There are a lot of people out there who are "by the book" and perhaps the INTJ is on board with that to a point – but the INTJ is also willing to chuck the book if it's getting in their way, and they are willing to enact bold means for a necessary end, the point where it might alarm their coworkers and supervisors.

INTJs are known for their:

## Thinking

Consistent use of logic doesn't mean that INTJs can't be coaxed out of a certain way of thinking; it just means that they will always approach a problem with the same impersonal method, regardless of the outcome, like a scientist performing an experiment but changing a few variables to see what difference it makes. The basic principle is still the same, but the inquisitive INTJ will gladly accept varying results. So although INTJs can often be labeled as "robotic" or even "insensitive" because their choices are not generally based on their own emotions or the emotions of those around them, this shouldn't suggest that they are rigid and unbending. Far from it. But if you want to change an INTJs mind, you had best have the proof, the facts, the data to back it up, because that is what they value and that is what they consider when making decisions, at work or anywhere else.

## Judging

Judging types are motivated by goals and deadlines, making them extremely efficient and organized. These traits will obviously bode well in any professional career, but they serve especially well in the science fields that INTJs tend to gravitate toward, where the goals and deadlines may vary, but the ultimate prize tends to be that satisfying feeling of completion and accomplishment – at least fleetingly, before they move onto their next project. Still, while INTJs may seem single-minded in their dedication for a work assignment – indeed, all of their outward actions would suggest that they are choo-chooing along and neither hell nor high water will prevent them from making the station on time – inwardly there is flexibility, especially when it comes to new ideas and the exact method for accomplishing those dearly-held tasks by deadline.

Despite all the wonders that INTJs are capable of, there are some jobs which should surely be avoided for everyone's sakes. Examples of these include:

## Museum Tour Guides

Woe be unto the poor soul who tries to correct the INTJ who could only find a position as a museum tour guide. Fiercely protective of their own correctness in most matters, the INTJ is also not what you would call a "people person," and if someone really did try to speak up and add to their tour guide's commentary – even worse, with false information – they could expect a razor-sharp put-down filled with bristling animosity from an individual who is frankly sick and tired of dealing with the public's ignorance.

## Models

There are definitely models out there who use their earnings and success to jumpstart more intellectual careers, but you likely wouldn't find any INTJs using the job as a springboard to anything. Modeling requires a certain degree of people-pleasing, not to mention tact (unless you're Naomi Campbell), plus tedious hours of hair and make-up at runway shows and shoots, and despite their varied schedules and international travel, those bright spots simply aren't going to be enough for the INTJ to find anything worthwhile in the profession.

## Nursing Home Aide

While INTJs probably love and admire their parents and grandparents, working around others' – particularly those who are in need of a lot of nurturing – would not be a great fit. The social nature of the job would be a stretch for INTJs to begin with, but nursing home aides also require a lot of empathy and compassion – two emotion-based traits that the INTJ may have, but does not necessarily engage in his interaction with others. Instead, INTJs prefer to "help" others in need by giving them the most thoroughly logical answer to their problems that is possible. Not really what you're looking for in the person attending your sweet old grandmother recovering from hip surgery.

INTJs clearly are not overly-emotional, nurturing/empathic sorts, and they need work that constantly challenges them and stretches their broad intellect. There are so many jobs out there that require the INTJ touch, and while they might not be affecting lives the way a social worker might, these personality types are improving society by offering technological innovation and social stability. Here are some of the amazing careers where INTJs work their special brand of magic.

# 1. Astrophysicist

**The Introvert Advantage:** Astrophysics isn't exactly a light-hearted topic and scholars must go through rigorous schooling. Only those with stellar – no pun intended – grades in math and sciences at the undergraduate level should even consider going into the field for graduate and post-graduate studies. The level of thinking necessary in astrophysics is astonishing, and those who devote their lives to this study – and study they do, as well as writing – are far and few. But that is what draws INTJs to it in the first place – that singularity, the specialness and knowing that they are likely working in an environment where independence is vital.

**The Intuitive Advantage:** There couldn't be a more "intuitive" profession than theoretical astrophysics, which is one of two major branches of the subject. Theoretical astrophysics takes the known information about the cosmos and proposes educated theories about all sorts of different things related to space (for instance, what a star was like billions of years ago). New and innovative ideas, thinking outside of the box (while keeping in mind the known theories and properties of astrophysics), understanding the big picture and not being afraid of what is abstract or unknown – these are all excellent qualities that INTJs bring to the table.

**The Thinking Advantage:** Despite Anne Hathaway's impassioned speech about love in the 2014 hit Interstellar, love – and other emotions of that nature – has very little to do with science and space. This is just as well for INTJs, who by their own admission prefer to make their decisions based on sound logic, weighing the known facts and not letting personal preferences, or the preferences of others, interfere. Even when dealing with something as abstract as theoretical astrophysics, INTJs can be counted upon to reach their conclusions based on what has already been proved or what can be proved – though they may pursue answers based on an informed hunch.

**The Judging Advantage:** Despite the truly awesome scope of what is being studied, astrophysics is still a science and, as such, basic principles and rules still apply. This is just fine for the INFJ, whose judgment aspect responds well to limits and thrives on organization (at least outwardly – inside, the INTJ astrophysicist might not care so much if a paper is turned in by deadline, but the overall need for it to ensure that the job is done well motivates them to do get it done). Full-time careers in astrophysics are difficult to come by because of the low turnover rate, so a capable approach is key.

# 2. Biotechnology Researcher

**The Introvert Advantage:** Like many of the other sciences, biotechnology – which is the study of plants and animals at the molecular level, including their cells and DNA, so that the information gleaned can be used to help humans in a variety of ways – can be an isolated endeavor. There are classes at the undergrad level, first-year bio courses filled with students, but by the graduate and post-graduate stages, the herd is thinned down to individuals serious about their work, which often involves long hours studying and reading. INTJs are well-suited to this environment, though, whether it's for a class or in the lab.

**The Intuitive Advantage:** Great breakthroughs in science and technology are often caused by hunches that are pursued, usually to the dismay or outrage of others (look at Masters and Johnson, who pioneered sexual research in the 1950s; Dr. William Masters, as portrayed by Michael Sheen on Showtime's *Masters of Sex* is a strong contender for an INTJ personality type!). Yet INTJ hunches are rarely just a random feeling from their gut, as they might be for other personality types. They are usually well-informed by the type's vast database of knowledge, yet it is their intuitive willingness to embrace new ideas that turns their hunches into action.

**The Thinking Advantage:** INTJ biotechnology researchers are doing work that contributes to society's common good – for instance, developing disease and pestilence-resistant plants that are immune to the insect epidemics that can wipe out the crops we eat – but they generally are not, in typical thinking manner, motivated on the job by particularly altruistic feelings, nor do they let their emotions or the emotions of others influence their decisions. This can be important, particularly as the use of animals for testing may be necessary, or because of the growing furor over genetically modified foods, which some believe to be unethical.

**The Judging Advantage:** Scientists must handle everything they do with the utmost precision, and the INTJs judgment aspect is very influential in this way. Furthermore, their judging trait is what allows them to exist harmoniously, as they are apt to plan ahead and then follow that plan through, in a methodical and strategic way which is beneficial to exacting protocols. They can easily make a list of tasks that they must accomplish, particularly in the lab, and then check each one off, so that everything that needs to be done is not only done well, it is done on time.

# 3. Business Accountant

**The Introvert Advantage:** Business accountants deal with mathematics – numbers and formulas and also computer software – and they act as personal financial managers for businesses big and small. This is no easy task; records of costs and cash flow can be as unwieldy to accountants in the same way that ungrammatical essays appear to English professors. It takes a lot of time and concentration to put these things to rights for a company or develop an accounting system, but INTJs prefer to work alone and embrace this type of career, where they often have the option of closing their office door and shutting out the noise.

**The Intuitive Advantage:** Part of the business accountant's job is to come up with a system for bookkeeping (it is then the bookkeeper's job, if there is one, to manage the day-to-day numbers). The overall system might be a general one that many different companies can use, but certain parts must be tweaked and personalized for each specific entity. The INTJ's intuitive knack for problem-solving, along with her gift for seeing a big picture and analyzing it thoroughly, enables her to come up with efficient solutions that are tailor-made for the business, keeping in mind its weaknesses and it strengths, so that profit can be increased with each passing month.

**The Thinking Advantage:** So how does the accountant decide what are a company's strengths and weaknesses? That is where the thinking aspect comes in, because this logic-based trait enables INTJs to weigh values objectively. It also informs that anal-retentive tic in them that, when taking in something for the first time, lets them immediately identify the flaw. And unlike their feeling counterparts, INTJs have no problem pointing out inconsistencies, because they believe they are just doing their job and – after all – they're not getting paid to mince words or soften the truth.

**The Judging Advantage:** Accountants must be, well, accountable – they have to be reliable, organized and on-task. Businesses are normally relying on them not only to manage their financials, but to file their taxes with the IRS – meaning they must prepare the tax reports on time and factually. This government agency isn't prone to leniency in the event of a mistake, so INTJs must be exceptionally devoted to their work, knowing the business's financial inside and out – and they usually do, because it is encoded in their DNA to succeed.

# 4. Business Consultant

**The Introvert Advantage:** Admittedly, the role of business consultant – where someone is hired as part of a firm or individually to assess the performance of a business and see how it could be managed more smoothly and efficiently – might not be for every INTJ, because there is a strong focus on people skills. However, these skills are not so much "getting along" as they are "being able to effectively communicate an idea." They might not need to speak with everyone in the company; their dealings may be confined to the upper management, unless someone seems particularly out of line in the cubicles.

**The Intuitive Advantage:** When you look at people who have built incredibly powerful and world-changing businesses – like Bill Gates, who is more extraverted, but clearly has the intuitive aspect to his personality – you notice a pattern of people who pushed the limits of what was thought possible. This is because they didn't stop innovating just because no one else had done something before, and it's this very trait in the INTJ that makes them so well-suited to shaking things up in a business – even if their ideas seem a little "out there" at first – and turning the company into its most productive incarnation.

**The Thinking Advantage:** Often in business, hard decisions must be made, and they must be made swiftly. This can include the firing of a long-time employee because of their bloated or the acquisition of a small family-owned business that is fighting to its last breath to resist. Business consultants have to make a lot of decisions that aren't personal, but might feel as though they are. In this instance, they are well-equipped, backed up by their certainty in facts and figures that they advising the right thing– because after all, they were hired to make the company start turning a profit again.

**The Judging Advantage:** Anyone who is consulting with businesses must know how to run one themselves, and to do that they will need a strong judging aspect. In the arts, you can get away with spontaneity and a free-wheeling lifestyle, but to run a company – and to shoulder the responsibility of others' livelihoods – you need a more stable personality, and that is what the INTJs have. Not only are they themselves organized and efficient, but good business consultants can teach their clients the same, using their creativity to come up with exercises that make the lessons stick.

# 5. Campaign Manager

**The Introvert Advantage:** It's true, there are usually a lot of people involved in a campaign, but the INTJ who has been bitten by the political bug will shine in the position of campaign manager – after all, most of the limelight (or harsh criticism) is going to focused on the politician whose campaign they are holding together. Besides, managers can delegate tasks, and the contemplative and penetrating INTJ can gather around him a group of trusted individuals who are competent (really, the highest praise anyone can get from an INTJ) and hard-working. INTJs will also be prone to developing close working relationships with their politician clients.

**The Intuitive Advantage:** If you were to follow the trajectory of a single campaign – like say, that of Elizabeth Warren, when she ran for the U.S. Senate seat in Massachusetts in 2012 – you would see twists and turns, conflicts and resolutions, truly ugly moments and ones that are, well, rather beautiful to behold. The point being, campaigns are unpredictable and bumpy, but the intuitive nature of the INTJ campaign manager is one that allows for constant reevaluation of information, so that what seemed like bad news yesterday is, at the hands of a capable INTJ, given a new, positive angle tomorrow.

**The Thinking Advantage:** Much like in businesses, campaigns have to be run like well-oiled machines. The modern political campaign is hugely expensive – and then there's the small matter of the politician's reputation on the line throughout the entire process. This means campaign managers have to take care of their "product" – the candidate – with the same devotion that a small business owner has for his brainchild, and so sometimes ruthless decisions must be made. When the INTJ weighs the pros and cons, as he is wont to do, and finds that the less friendly option is the most expedient, you can bet expediency wins every time.

**The Judging Advantage:** Managing a candidate's schedule is practically a job on its own, yet that is part of the campaign manager's responsibility, as well as coordinating the efforts of all the staff members. The INTJ campaign manager is lucky in that he is naturally prone to distributing tasks in an analytical fashion, ensuring that everyone is doing what he or she is supposed to be (with consideration made for who would do what best), and no one makes a misstep that could cost the candidate the election. "Failing" is not part of an INTJ's vocabulary, and they are formidably equipped to avoid that fate.

# 6. City Planner

**The Introvert Advantage:** While city planners are often working in public offices, the offices themselves are usually not incredibly busy places, and the planners generally don't have to deal with an excessive number of people, and they aren't forced by rote to make a lot of small talk (unless the office gossip waylays them before lunch). There is, in fact, a lot of time spent analyzing information and producing reports, tasks whose drudgery are mitigated by the fact that the work involved makes a real difference in developing urban areas by promoting green space and equitable distribution of city wealth to all neighborhoods.

**The Intuitive Advantage:** There are a lot of factors which must be taken into account when preparing a report; often, planners will do a decent amount of traveling to meet with city officials for areas they are studying, and they will take notes which must be synthesized with known facts and figures. Then, from that information planners – usually working in small teams – must decide how best to allocate resources of time, money and materials to bring the city into the modern times. There is a lot of problem-solving needed, but no one is better equipped for that task than the INTJ.

**The Thinking Advantage:** City planning is as detailed and precise as any of the physical sciences, and when there are multiple solutions – each with their own positives and negatives – it is up to the INTJ city planner to decide which choice to follow. They are probably well aware that what they choose could have reverberating effects for generations to come, but instead of ruling with their heart – for a surety, INTJs know what option they would pick if it were up to them – they will always pick the way that best marries the values the city's leaders have chosen as the most important.

**The Judging Advantage:** When the word "planning" is right there in the job title, there is no way around the fact that a judging personality is going to best meet the needs of the profession. Judging INTJs are just the sort to look at a project as a whole and decide ahead of time how to pace the progress. They have an innate sense of what should go when, so that each individual aspect of the entire project is completed at the best stage in the assignmen.. And because nothing matters more to municipalities than staying on budget, INTJ planners will have thought ahead for that, too.

# 7. Climatologist

**The Introvert Advantage:** Some scientists might be more visible or their job might be more sociable in nature, but climatology isn't a huge field – though it is hugely important – and it's not a "trendy" science, despite the clear uptick in interest in environmentalism. Climatology blends the independence of research with the intellectualism of paper and report writing, and it's a good choice to INTJs who are interested in studying how climate affects humans and vice versa. Social engagements are blessedly rare (confined usually to oral reports), while inquisition and the independent pursuit of knowledge and answers is encouraged.

**The Intuitive Advantage:** As in all sciences, a curious mind who is open to new ideas and is always absorbing information not before processed is a boon, but because climatology in this day and age is so vitally important to the continuance of the human race on this planet, problem solving is especially significant, and the INTJ's ability to tap into his intuitive aspect and embrace solutions – no matter how non-traditional they might be – makes him an asset in the field and probably a rock star among colleagues. That kind of "thinking outside the box" is also very inspirational for others.

**The Thinking Advantage:** Despite their innovative suggestions for problem solving, INTJs still arrive at their conclusions by way of careful observation and weighing of the known facts and theories. This only means that nay-sayers who might have a beef with the INTJ's suggestions – and there are many out there who would argue on this contentious topic – will arrive at a wall of factual and well-founded information that is difficult to rebut. Which is, incidentally, exactly how INTJs like to play the game, and while it might be construed as arrogant, at least it's based on unbiased science.

**The Judging Advantage:** A climatologist's schedule can be surprisingly busy, especially if he makes trips out to the field to look at ice that's hundreds of thousands of years old, and he has to sneak that in between the winter and spring sessions at the school where he teaches. But the INTJ's propensity for planning over the long-term stands him in good stead professionally, ensuring that the different pieces of his career run forward smoothly and nothing has to be rushed or done at the last minute (although it's fair to say the INTJ has planned for that instance, too).

# 8. Computer Scientist

**The Introvert Advantage:** A career in computer science may land the employee in an office or research lab, but the work is mostly independent. They may work collaboratively in teams on occasion, but each individual will have his or her own assignment, and they will be expected to work on it mostly alone – left alone – and probably physically isolated at a work station or even a private office (for those higher up on the food chain). The isolation is necessary because INTJ computer scientists need plenty of space – both physically and mentally – to think up the next great innovation that will change everything.

**The Intuitive Advantage:** Computer scientists, whether they're working as researches for a university or have been hired as employees at a cutting-edge tech company, are always innovating, always creating. They are pushing the envelope and the boundaries of what is possible. INTJs are perfectly suited to this task because their intuitive minds – which are always pushing concepts forward – blend analytical mastery with a desire to see their projects through to some kind of physical, working creation. This isn't necessarily true of all intuitive personalities, but the INTJ is especially concerned with making his ideas accessible.

**The Thinking Advantage:** Thinking types are not just thinking; they are analyzing and classifying and doing all those great things that make scientists so vitally important to society. It takes a truly unique individual to find joy in pursuing technology to the advanced level of a computer scientist, but the INTJ's personality is ideally synthesized with the skills necessary for this field, and we need the thinking aspect to find that one flaw in the software that is prohibiting it from working perfectly. Where others might be dismayed by the task, INTJs savor the challenge.

**The Judging Advantage:** A methodical approach is necessary when dealing with something as complex as computer science. While it may look like a muddled mess of codes to the untrained eye, actually everything that constitutes computer science is formulated and routine. While the INTJ may be able to think in abstract terms, he is comfortable acting according to more regimented regulations. He always keeps in mind the "science" part of computer science – that everything happens for a reason because brilliant minds have spent lifetimes creating systems based on patterns.

# 9. Dermatologist

**The Introvert Advantage:** Dermatologists are doctors who help people with skin problems. This can be as simple as more severe forms of acne or venture into far more serious territory with chronic or recurring diseases. Medical school is a given, so candidates interested in becoming dermatologists must be prepared to give up a significant portion of their young adulthood to study – something INTJs generally don't mind, since they prefer introverted activities anyway. Medical offices may be busy, but doctors interact with patients one-on-one, so INTJs can keep small talk to a minimum as they dig in to help find the cause of the skin problem.

**The Intuitive Advantage:** Like any medical profession, sometimes symptoms are mysterious. It's up to the doctor to perform thorough investigations, through interviews and lab tests and by combing through her extensive learning and prior experience. There are a lot of components involved in diagnosing even a simple skin ailment, but intuitive INTJs like gathering all of the facts and solving the problem, even if it means taking a non-traditional approach now and then. While their judging aspect might suggest to the outside world that INTJs are rigid on the rules, their intuitive trait keeps their minds more open and flexible.

**The Thinking Advantage:** Still, in medicine it is best to perform the established, necessary steps, in order, before branching out into more abstract theories, and this is what the thinking INTJ will do, drawing upon her considerable wealth of knowledge and her faith that protocol exists for a reason – because it works. Doctors sometimes earn a reputation for being "uncaring" or "insensitive," but INTJ dermatologists who come across this way do care – they care so much that they want to solve the problem with the maximum amount of efficiency possible, even if it means halting tearful stories and focusing on present symptoms.

**The Judging Advantage:** Dermatologists often open private practices, which means skin treatment is their business – and they are small business owners, with all the same responsibilities as someone who sells handmade yo-yos. Having a keen inclination for organization is important, as is preparedness and planning ahead – sometimes even years in advance. Whereas their perceiving counterparts would be hesitant to sign a lease that locks them into one spot for a few years, the judging INTJs will have already weighed their options and have no problem putting their John Hancock on the dotted line.

# 10. Economist

**The Introvert Advantage:** Economists tend to work in more specific careers – like journalism, teaching, financial planning, stock trading or law – but they get to add "economist" to their resumes or CVs because they publish on the subject of the economy or may be interviewed as an expert, and they are widely recognized as authorities on the topic. As with any significant writing or appearance that contributes intelligently to a conversation, this requires the economist to be well-read, well-written and well-spoken, three traits which the INTJ easily encompasses because he is, by his very nature, a thoughtful, contemplative soul.

**The Intuitive Advantage:** The dizzying world of American and global economics is staggeringly complex, but INTJs are equipped to master the complexities because of the enormous capacity of their brains to break down the chaos, which gives them a rare advantage other personality types. Sometimes the economy does unpredictable things, but the INTJ has the penetrating insight to find the cause before anyone else. They might get taken by surprise, but they won't be blind in the dark for too long, no matter how unique or rare the situation, and that will make them the answers people and the people who can turn things around.

**The Thinking Advantage:** Economics, like other sciences, has very little room for personal preferences or biases, so it is important that the economist's feelings not sway their opinions. Further, despite the current state of American economics, it is even better if politics can be left out, and instead we focus on bipartisan solutions for economic failures. Though the INTJ is often very opinionated (and not shy about expressing that), he is also among the most sensible and well-reasoned thinkers out there, able to put aside his own prejudices – or any of those near to him – in favor of the best choice and the best plan to move progress along.

**The Judging Advantage:** Economists are often like weathermen in the sense that they provide an important forecast by which others prepare. They themselves must prepare for the future, though in their case it can mean readying a scholarly article while teaching three courses at a university or directly helping seniors make the most of their savings by judging, to the best of their ability, what investments will provide security in the years to come. There is often enormous pressure, and the stakes are quite high when it comes to people's money, but INTJs have an intuition when it comes to financial storms or sun.

# 11. Oncology Researcher

**The Introvert Advantage:** More than ever oncology – the study of cancer – has become an important and integral part of the medicinal landscape in the U.S. and beyond. Researchers form an absolutely essential part of that study, because they are the ones discovering breakthroughs in treatment. Oncology researchers are classically trained doctors who specialize in oncology with particular expertise in areas like genetics or immunology. Their working conditions generally constitute a laboratory, where their days are spent in relative seclusion with other researchers, an ideal setting for INTJs who may crave some social interaction, but only to bounce ideas off other like-minded individuals.

**The Intuitive Advantage:** Oncology research is more than just mindless testing and re-testing; successful researchers are an elite class of medical doctors who have proven that they have the creativity to stop the spread of cancer and prohibit it from returning to the human body. Can the average person go into an oncology lab and come up with a way to make cancer treatments less frightening for children? Certainly not. There are two parts to oncology research which must marry: the scientific know-how and the innovation to imagine new ways of manipulating what is already known or pursuing new knowledge.

**The Thinking Advantage:** Bleeding heart Feelers beware: medical research is probably not your cup of tea. Animals like rats and other small rodents are often used – that is, injected with illnesses – in order to develop cures for humans. INTJs may not, deep down, care for the fact that animals must be used to develop cures and treatments, but you can bet if it will stop a human from dying an untimely and painful death, they will do it because it is what needs to be done. Putting aside personal biases in favor of what is logical – saving human lives – is the INTJ from head to toe.

**The Judging Advantage:** Researchers must obtain funding, and funding must be applied for in long, drawn-out processes that can take months, if not years of planning. Enter the INTJ, who is naturally in it for the long haul and willing to commit to a lot of hard work and paper pushing for the sake of her research and the lives at stake. Her research in general is a study in long-term planning and goal setting, getting things done item by item and not being able to move forward until one phase is complete. It takes a measured patience that INTJs who are saving the world have in abundance.

# 12. Librarian

**The Introvert Advantage:** Professional librarians don't just work in a library for a few years and then magically gain certification. Students from all backgrounds, but especially English and other arts must go to an accredited school for a Masters in Library Science degree before they can begin to apply for jobs in public, private or university libraries. It is intense scholarly work that can be isolating and require plenty of alone time, but introverted INTJs don't mind. Further, librarians on the job do work among the public, but the tasks required are nowhere near as demanding socially as, say, a retail job or a bartending position.

**The Intuitive Advantage:** Librarians actually spend more time problem solving than you might think, particularly those who work in library management. Aside from putting books on shelves after people return them (the typical idea most people have of librarian work), they perform a dynamic array of duties including cataloging, classifying, preserving and archiving. They want to provide their library's books and other services in the most appealing and user-friendly way possible, so INTJs will find that libraries make use of their creativity and inherent management skills, on a daily basis and in an atmosphere that promotes learning and new ideas.

**The Thinking Advantage:** INTJs who may have a more highly developed feeling aspect along with their thinking traits will do well in libraries where they can help people who are looking to them as authorities in research. But their strictly thinking aspect is a boon in a field where technicalities and small details matter, because a library runs on a very strict system that allocates each book to its own place, videos to another and magazines and periodicals somewhere else. Further, archives often contain important, significant historical documents which require robotic attention and care for the sake of their future preservation.

**The Judging Advantage:** What is wonderful about the INTJ personality in a library is that when things don't always go according to plan INTJs have the flexibility internally to accept the blip and keep rolling, yet outwardly, they are still task-oriented and stick to the plan as best they can, providing the kind of stability needed to keep such incredible institutions of learning and literature open for generations to come. Libraries seem like ancient artifacts to some, but they are an essential part of any community or university and INTJ librarians are the ones who will ensure they remain so.

# 13. Mathematician

**The Introvert Advantage:** Mathematicians put truth to the lie that you won't use that college algebra in the real world. In fact, mathematicians use all kinds of math – most of it highly advanced – in the same way that engineers use physics to create new inventions and advance society technologically. This career tract emphasizes the intellect and deep, meaningful thought, and mathematicians can choose whether they prefer to work in an environment that is more face-paced or slower. This is a good feature for INTJs who fall all over the introverted spectrum (some more so than others) and may desire varying degrees of socializing.

**The Intuitive Advantage:** Thinking about the future and what it could be possible to achieve: that is what intuitive personality types do, and that is what mathematicians do as part of their day-in, day-out routine at work. These aren't fusty, cardigan-wearing nerds in glasses – these are seriously brilliant geniuses who are working in exciting and dynamic fields, using their skill with numbers to help push technology to the cutting edge. The mathematician career might as well be tailor-made for the INTJ, because concepts, innovation and problem-solving are her bread and butter and the reason she gets up in the morning.

**The Thinking Advantage:** Patterns are the touchstone of mathematics. Patterns symbolize order and stability. The thinking INTJ values these characteristics as an innate part of herself, and she is more than happy to apply her natural gift for patterns with government agencies, universities and private companies that produce work in the sciences. Her quick and analytical mind can easily sift through known facts for useful information and along the way pick up flaws or discrepancies in data, making her an essential and valuable member of any team that is trying to improve technology or our understanding of principles.

**The Judging Advantage:** It makes sense that INTJs would have a natural propensity for mathematics – it is a field which deals in and rewards organization and control, and the judging personality types, especially those combined with the thinking aspect, gravitate toward careers such as that like a moth to candlelight. Mathematics, like other sciences, require long-term planning and commitment to intense, sometimes life-consuming projects which have many stages that must be completed in their proper order. Perceiving types would flee at the hint of such a notion, but INTJs are perfectly at home.

# 14. Military Strategist

**The Introvert Advantage:** Competent military strategists, who are highly in demand, though there is not a lot of turnover in the field, will commonly work with like-minded individuals who are probably less interested in chit-chat (relief, to the introvert!) and more involved in protecting and deploying troops in a meaningful and effective way overseas – and other matters related to the efficient running of a modern military that is always on the cutting edge of technology and leads the world in spending. Specialized strategist programs through the U.S military are rigorous and demanding, while on-the-job duties require strong communication skills, which introverts tend to have – they just don't waste them on small talk.

**The Intuitive Advantage:** Running a military is one thing; running a military effectively is quite another. Strategists not only consider troops in battle or who are stationed around the world, they look within their own organization to identify the most efficient way to run the "business" – rather like managers – and they must be open to changes in how that is done in order to maximize resources of time, money and man power. The INTJ is well-suited to this kind of position because he is an outstanding ideas person who isn't afraid to admit when something isn't working and then find a solution that will do better.

**The Thinking Advantage:** Highly developed logic is necessary in the logistics of planning effective military strategy. But there is more to the job. A lot of the time orders are coming from higher up, and strategists may not agree with them – but it is their job to comply with the instructions that are given or they will find themselves checking the want-ads. Because INTJs have well-tuned thinking aspects, they can put their own personal feelings aside and just do their job to the best of their ability.

**The Judging Advantage:** Move and counter-move. If you have ever played chess or Risk, then you know that it's the long game that matters. Consider Queen Elizabeth I's "secretary of state," William Cecil. He was her closest confidant and chief military advisor, and he spun out webs of intrigue that would take years to reach fruition, but he had the patience and the foresight (and he helped usher in England's Golden Age). In matters of state and military strategy, planning is important, but INTJs are also always looking ahead. If their current plan is failing, their response is to create a new one. They are surprisingly flexible while remaining stolidly reliable.

# 15. Nuclear Engineer

**The Introvert Advantage:** The vast amounts of schooling alone would fell lesser personalities, but INTJs are more or less programmed to embrace long hours spent in seclusion, studying the necessary principles needed to understand one of the world's most exciting and dangerous topics: nuclear engineering. As a nuclear engineer, INTJs must work alongside other people quite frequently, but these like-minded individuals are just as focused and enthusiastic – no one wanders into nuclear engineering by accident. As introverted personalities, INTJs are skilled communicators who can say what they need to say in between bouts of independent work.

**The Intuitive Advantage:** Nuclear engineers are always trying to use what they know to make the world's technology even better and more efficient, or they are pursuing new ideas to develop and add to the canon of knowledge. Rather than being putting off by jargon and complex theories, INTJs are born to run with it, and their enthusiasm for the field is what makes our world such an amazing place to live in – if there weren't people like INTJs who would readily and happily study applications of nuclear energy, we wouldn't have such widespread electricity and our lakes and oceans would be polluted with hazardous wastes.

**The Thinking Advantage:** Nuclear engineers are highly educated, and they more often than not choose to get Master's or doctorate degrees. This means a lot of math and a lot of physics, but INTJs tend to love these topics anyway, because – like a sound logical argument – they just make sense. A solution is either a solution or it isn't, and tough-minded INTJs aren't going to cut corners in order to be the first to discover a new technology. Their integrity simply won't allow for it, and the fact that the math might be fudged would probably destroy them worse, emotionally, than a horrible break-up.

**The Judging Advantage:** As with all sciences, nuclear engineering takes foresight and commitment to long-term projects. Engineers have to be able (and willing) to start with one small seed of an idea, yet look forward, years into the future. It takes a small village to turn a single idea into a reality, and that means a lot of dedication, hard work, planning and organization, but the INTJ scientist's strong judging core is thrilled to be a part of something that is so outwardly static but so inwardly dynamic and open to new possibilities.

# 16. Physics Professor

**The Introvert Advantage:** University functions aside, introverted INTJs who are teaching physics at the college level can at least be counted upon to think up some clever ways of making their coursework interesting for students. While INTJs tend to be stand-offish and aloof, students who come to office hours for help will likely get to see a more relaxed and joking side of their mysterious instructor. Colleagues who get close may be more like-minded in terms of personality, but they will find a trustworthy and loyal coworker who would make a good chair of the department if no one else want the job.

**The Intuitive Advantage:** Physics may deal with matters that can be touched and seen, but the math and science behind it can be frustratingly theoretical, and it can be especially difficult for young students to understand. As mentioned, INTJs are innovators with a penchant for making lessons interesting and for explaining complexities in a way which resonates with students. It is not enough for an INTJ to understand a theory herself; she in a teaching position has taken the natural INTJ "next step" toward making the knowledge accessible for all, and she has the passionate and curious creativity to bring that to the classroom.

**The Thinking Advantage:** Tough but fair: that's how students will think of their INTJ physics professor. She isn't there to coddle people in her classroom, but she will make a special appointment outside of her office hours with a student who is struggling, provided that individual is showing an earnest enthusiasm to learn. Actually, the world needs more thinking professors – these are the types who prepare teenagers and young 20-somethings for the real world, where lame excuses and lies are easily exposed and emotions often have to be set aside in pursuit of truth and fact.

**The Judging Advantage:** If you have never prepared lesson plans or a syllabus, stay away. Many teachers can tack on 20+ hours to their work weeks because of the planning necessary to make the courses the best they can be. The (let's face it) over-achieving INTJ isn't content to have a good class; she wants to have the best physics class, the one where students walk away with their minds blown open by all the incredible stuff they're learning, and that takes a lot of advanced consideration, from the books students will read, to the assignments which will be graded, to the writing of exams.

# 17. Private Investigator

**The Introvert Advantage:** If you thought private investigators were relegated to spy novels, think again. INTJs will find the job appealing because it's incredibly independent if they prefer – they can work on a kind of "freelance" basis, taking on clients who seek their services. And it's not all action, although there is plenty of that (not quite up to the level of films, of course, but it's certainly more dynamic than a desk job somewhere). Private investigators and detectives have to be able to think hard in order to make connections and draw informed conclusions, and INTJs can do that with aplomb.

**The Intuitive Advantage:** As mentioned, investigating requires a lot of dot-connection and following of leads, and it is incredibly unfair to other personality types – yet wonderfully advantageous to clients – that INTJs dominate in this area, both because of their ability to keep the "big picture" in mind (often, people get lost in the details) and because they are wired to think logically. Yet their intuitive aspect also gives them insight into the unpredictability of human nature, which is very important when one needs to consider why someone has done something that seems completely random.

**The Thinking Advantage:** Cheating spouses. Kidnapped children. Fraud committed in the name of love. It's all very powerful, emotional stuff, and it could be easy to get sucked in and then taken in by beguiling suspects who put on Oscar-winning performances lamenting their bad childhoods or tragic circumstances. Those tears go to naught with INTJ investigators, who may inwardly feel a seed of compassion but will squash it in order to do their job. Investigators can't make a living if they are falling prey to talented sociopaths or letting personal biases get in the way.

**The Judging Advantage:** Running an investigation, whether it's a team of FBI agents or a single man tracking down leads to find the whereabouts of a lost child, takes planning and organization that INTJs have in abundance. What's more, their interior flexibility helps them avoid the rigidity that could plague other personality types, so that if a plan goes awry in a heartbeat, instead of wringing his hands over the lost opportunity, the INTJ investigator uses his brilliant mind to implement a new strategy that takes into account ground lost or new information gained.

# 18. Security Analyst

**The Introvert Advantage:** Analyzing anything takes a serious amount of concentration, but security is especially important in this vast cyber-centric world. Security analysts can work in a variety of different sectors, from government agencies to private firms, but there is no denying the enhanced intellect needed to be a successful analyst and the long hours that need to be spent developing and maintaining security systems that will keep sensitive information safe from a hostile outside world. INTJs are naturally drawn to positions which require extensive thought, so security analysis is a great fit.

**The Intuitive Advantage:** Drawing upon multiple disciplines, including IT problem solving and business administration, is a practice for which INTJ analysts are well-equipped. They are uniquely gifted in the race to solve the problems that face companies in need of cyber security. This is because keeping information secure is a multi-dimensional problem that must be approached in perpetually new and innovative ways, because the bad guys out there – hackers and the like – are getting smarter and are arming themselves better. Security has to evolve with it or sensitive company information – or even our personal information, given to these companies in confidence – could end up leaked, leaving us all vulnerable.

**The Thinking Advantage:** Despite the evolving nature of security analysis, certain factors will remain the same, and in some cases, it is the inconsistencies in the system that can alert an analyst to a vulnerability or an attack. INTJs are born to embrace patterns in math and computer science, and this makes them especially alert on the job – these logical, pattern-minded individuals will notice a blip on their computer screen the way art critics will automatically cringe at anatomical incorrectness. Companies with INTJ security analysts on their team can count on reliably quick take-downs of breaches and swift mitigation of security problems.

**The Judging Advantage:** Analyzing a company's cyber security system takes comprehensive foresight that the perceiving personality types simply don't have. INTJs' judging aspect puts them at a sound advantage when it comes to formulating far-reaching company-wide plans, implementing security measures and even training employees to recognize breaches in the system. It's not that INTJs want other people to do their jobs for them (far from it); but training everyone in the company to some extent in security protocol empowers them with knowledge, mitigates ignorance and works as a kind of pro-active preventative measure to keep information safe.

# 19. Statistician

**The Introvert Advantage:** If you dreaded your stats class in college, you are not alone, but INTJs were probably the know-it-alls in the front row, for whom the concepts came easily. Statisticians are much in demand in all manner of fields, including climatology, education, the healthcare system, finance and even football (who do you think crunches all the numbers for those player stats and makes educated forecasts for your fantasy players?). Because their ability to analyze data makes them so widely desirable, INTJs can have their pick of work environments, but often working independently or with small teams of competent coworkers.

**The Intuitive Advantage:** One of the most important considerations for the thought-based INTJ is the big picture – the larger truth. Statisticians use numbers to get at larger truths, whether it's a graph showing the overall $CO_2$ emissions output versus worldwide average temperature spike or a sportscaster's analysis telling fans which quarterback everyone should be trying to draft for their fantasy football team. INTJs will make use of the smaller bits of information, but they serve as means to an ambitious end. INTJ statisticians want to show the general public that a lot of their preconceived notions are wrong and they have the facts to back it up.

**The Thinking Advantage:** Getting at the truth, at the big picture, can sometimes be ugly. Everything we know about the Holocaust is based on carefully researched facts, and it takes a certain kind of historian to have the courage to say, "I know this will upset people, but the truth needs to be told." It is much the same for statisticians, who are using their immense talent for logic and data analysis to serve up truths which are often unpalatable and may even end up subjected to harsh criticism. Yet INTJs refuse to put others' discomfort above telling the world what it needs to hear.

**The Judging Advantage:** Statisticians may "go into the office," but a lot of them actually get to conduct studies (and from the studies, glean the statistics that they use to generate new, factual information). Sometimes studies will be shorter affairs, a few months of work, but larger, more ambitious projects can take years of dedication. Perceiving types resist being locked into schedules, but INTJs take comfort in knowing what they are going to be doing a week from now, a month from now or even years in the future. It's part of what makes them so successful and places them among the highest-earning personality types.

# 20. Tax Attorney

**The Introvert Advantage:** If you have ever watched a film or TV show featuring an even remotely realistic depiction of lawyers (on your way, Ally McBeal), then you probably saw them trading sharp barbs with other lawyers before going home to an empty house, maybe a cat. Law can be an especially lonely and isolating field, owing to the amount of work necessary, and even though attorneys work in firms and teams within firms, the amount of independence is still quite high. Further, attorneys are expected to spend time alone, perusing paperwork, so the career is a good fit for INTJs.

**The Intuitive Advantage:** Law is a complicated field to begin with, but tax law is one of the most complex. Tax law definitely requires the smooth handling of a confident, creative individual who knows what she is about as she effectively tackles tax road blocks. INTJs have a natural affinity for the science of numbers and the innovation required to come up with legal solutions to individuals' or business' problems. They must keep in mind local and state, as well as federal tax laws, but this information – which might be dizzyingly disjointed to others – can be integrated flawlessly by the mastermind INTJ.

**The Thinking Advantage:** Lawyers may find themselves in positions which test their sensibilities, but they know they are themselves bounden to the laws which they uphold, including attorney/client privilege, which protects the information shared between lawyers and clients. Tax law can be especially difficult to navigate where the human condition in concerned, because it often deals with sensitive money issues relating to business accounts, inheritances and the like. A tax lawyer may be enlisted to help out a friend who is dealing with an IRS audit, but she isn't going to lie for the friend, no matter how long they may have known each other.

**The Judging Advantage:** Tax attorneys must always think ahead, whether they are just beginning to handle a case or they are fully enmeshed in some kind of legal battle. Law can be a lot like the military, with move and counter-move, and you can bet that if there is a need for an attorney, there will be some push-pull between legal counsels. INTJs have the personality for commitment and organization, two traits that will serve them especially well in the legal profession, and they won't be afraid to take on a big case, nor will they jump ship if the process drags out over months. They are dedicated workers who won't back down from a challenge even if they want to.

# 21. Technical Writer

**The Introvert Advantage:** Technical or "tech" writers work in varying environments, but one of the benefits of the job, particularly for INTJs, is that companies may be looking for freelancers or remote hires. This means that lone-wolf INTJs in the tech writing field could work from home and make their own hours, or work in-office but find themselves largely left to their own devices. Now and then they can make use of their superior communication skills by talking with engineers or technicians for research, but generally, tech writers are in the same position that any writer can be found: head bent over a glowing screen, fingers at the keyboard, clacking away.

**The Intuitive Advantage:** The INTJ, whether from genuine love of sharing knowledge or enjoying the feeling of imparting superior knowledge on the ignorant, are particularly hepped up in life over taking complicated, complex theories and ideas and making them palatable to the everyday Joe. This is exactly what tech writers need to be able to do, and individuals who have science and tech backgrounds (or are able to quickly absorb and process technical information), combined with the literary gifts of Hemingway are both rare and much in-demand, but it should come as no surprise that INTJs shine in this career.

**The Thinking Advantage:** Having the ability to control unwieldy data and information and then mold it into readable, accessible prose is more formulated than you might think, and certainly INTJs can turn this writing exercise into a science (with a logical formula that other tech writers, if they're smart, will adopt). INTJs may not have that "common touch" or strong empathic desire to help others, but they do believe in the systematic override of ignorance by knowledge and fact. Their part of the environmental movement is describing why a particular nuclear plant's method for waste disposal is the cleanest.

**The Judging Advantage:** Tech writers work on fixed deadlines and may juggle multiple projects at once, but the trade-off is that this career is one of the best-paid writing jobs out there. Their perceiving cousins would likely rather stick to the meandering art of novel writing, but INTJs take deep satisfaction in setting personal work goals and then meeting each one, over the course of weeks, months or even years. While tech writing can be very independent, the careers with the best job security and pay are long-term, full-time positions that require decisive commitment to one company.

INTJs have a formidable reputation for brilliance and accomplishment, and any kind of "mastermind" persona may be further enhanced by their somewhat stand-offish personalities. They might be difficult to get to know in work settings – certainly, coworkers are going to have to earn the INTJ's trust and respect – but once colleagues gain admittance to that golden circle, they will find a bastion of wit, humor, good sense and dedication. While an INTJ might pop up in unexpected places – like a social work office that handles sensitive and emotional cases – for the most part they are going to gravitate toward sciences and math. And we can be glad of that, because that is where they are likely to do their best work for humanity, bettering lives by making the complex accessible and the complicated simple. To know an INTJ is to feel a little intimidation and a lot of fascinated awe.